A Thousand-and-One Nights
& Twenty-Four Days

Also by Josh Goldberg

A Beggar at the Door: Longer and Shorter Psalms

Eight Beggars: Concatenating Verses of Separation and Repair

A Thousand-and-One Nights & Twenty-Four Days

Josh Goldberg

Albion
Andalus

Boulder, Colorado

2020

*"The old shall be renewed,
and the new shall be made holy."*
— Rabbi Avraham Yitzhak Kook

Albion-Andalus Inc.
P. O. Box 19852
Boulder, CO 80308
www.albionandalus.com

Design and composition by Albion-Andalus Inc.

Cover image "Built Upon Broken Tablets", Charcoal, ink,
carbon, chalk on paper 17"x18" by Josh Goldberg.

ISBN: 978-1-7348750-1-0

Manufactured in the United States of America

Dedication
Para mi querida Anita

CONTENTS

ACKNOWLEDGMENTS

FOR HER ENCOURAGEMENT and love I wish to thank my wife Anita; and to my publisher Netanel Miles-Yépez for his expertise and patience in making this book a reality.

— J.G.

A Thousand-and-One Nights

The Hand Holds the Night by a Thread

Night-conscious. Striking a lunar nerve. An alchemy denying any literalism or one-sidedness. Freely mining, hotly heating, quickly smelting, forging and annealing; impatiently infusing, evacuating, coloring, mixing, distilling. Not to let it cool, not yet.

A pharmakon of image-words. Poison and remedy. States of soul. Events touched and seen. Corrosive, heavy, sweating yet salvific. Dreaming the poem along, a night song stammering. Demanding a perplexed contemplation so the image won't disappear into generality. Turning kaleidoscopic meaning-patterns. Rectifying a language that is one's own.

The night sea journey that begins at the edges. Not in the upper world of Day. Subterranean, self-sustaining, moving downhill to the protean darkness, to the black sun of our own roasting, the fierce heat of fine ash. A lunatic nigredo, a night radix deconstructing reason and logic urging instead fluidity and downflow. The world of archetypes, psyche, imaginal fields.

One need not be deterred by the proliferation of images or paths the lines may take. Seek inspiration in the unconstrained undulations, its disjunctive and separate geographies. Hyphenated, clipped, or complete each line is pure stream. Thoughts, observations, moods, emotions.

Preface to *A Thousand-and-One-Nights*

Here is not the place to say whether A Thousand-and-One-Nights unifies or dissociates the personality, maps any strata of the subconscious. The void has been sighted. The imaginal field of immanence as a functioning faculty where two or more distant realities are juxtaposed. The more naturally distant in time and space, the more suggestive.

Writing one or two lines each night careful that the automatic flux not forfeit authenticity. Ignoring what was produced the previous night to maintain the viridity of the images. The only "negotiation": continue the line the following night, if need be.

Single lines split and rejoined. Read together, apart, like fragments of an ancient text under a lunatic moon. Finding congruity in incongruity, intersecting overtones, unexpected changes in trajectory.

A double space disrupts the line between two or three images. Disruptions or markers of equivalence transition, pause, or contrast images allowing flexibility of meaning, a "similarity between dissimilar things" (Freud).

Each line pursues the illogical, hurls toward the ambivalence of possibility. Taut or loose, fragmented or isolated the line cut to minimalist precision. The struggle is "to sketch the flow that already exists intact in mind" (Kerouac). First thoughts, ecstatic ardor, non-discriminatory intoxication. Elude the controls of thought, logic, and propriety.

"Submission to everything, open, listening" (Kerouac). Utilitarian perceptions disoriented yet tangible. But not of an intellectual, rational order.

Pinwheels of grace-spun images rotating on their small hinges in a single line.

— J.G.

Night: torrential rain sweeps my
northernmost sea

Night: dark soul's mudslide my exposed
rock-face ragged-uncertainty

Night: trees whistle for birds sea
hunts the dark

Night: mute with soliloquies

Night: sky pimpled with stars above
death's mezzanine

Night: cold drawn to fever camp

Night: holds back morning god-blue rush

A Thousand-and-One-Nights

Night: drains radiance-paws like tarantula

Night: light spurts above garage panic-stricken
in screaming heat

Night: cold china skies discovers snow
between her legs

Night: copse of glum shadows swallow
familiar pain

Night: ward's sweetmeat ribbons gluttony's
last great churning

Nightfall: down-river dust-bushland house
almost stands

Night: plumb line into eye of madness

Josh Goldberg

Night: sleeping dog distills desire
devoid of hair

Night: end-day's long leash forecourt-sorrows

Night: spins down like sycamore seeds
swiftness of wind

Night: lacewings perfectly love you

Night: messages swell in throat bloody-joints
still-born words

Night: accidental smiles twill patterns of
broken cheeks

Night: hair of your name on the tongue

A Thousand-and-One-Nights

Night: grilled on open fire lips

of apprehensive lead

Night: eyes asphalt-nestled wince
eager feeding

Night: among tents of orchids lay-lines
of your palms

Night: wild tongue seizes dreadful motion
under perpendicular skies

Night: house licked-over suitable
to your raw edge

Night: picks hair from her forehead

Josh Goldberg

Night: foreign rhythms unravel
mountain fields

Night: in service of beryl and lanolin bean
and double joss.

Night: uncoiled dreams refused by Day

Night: latent heat from evergreen
cannot find offerings

Night: backward path of licorice eyes

Night: drifts homeward identifying shot
already heard

Night: builds rafts of snow upon great rivers

A Thousand-and-One-Nights

Night: rubs body with last heat of summer

Night: silken shadows stone trees in twilight
splatters of dawn

Night: dead silence seals soundlessly
doves of the heart

Night: wolf preaches to birds fruit
of liberation

Night: even crooked branches to be admired

Night: heaven and earth in my stomach eyes
to full moon

Night: hyphenated words break fingers

Josh Goldberg

Night: silhouette at your feet backbone
bends the void

Night: existence not limited to single act

Night: face in mirror too close to see

Night: burning fires thin tongue

Night: as herds of deer scatter dung

Night: breaks into pieces sun rounds eye

Night: darkness falls back on itself refuses
hostile dawns

Night: horizon no longer night but not yet day

A Thousand-and-One-Nights

Night: moonlit grasses follow direction
of wind

Night: your name written on water

Night: difficult to be good-wise-happy

Night: simple wish penetrate stars

Night: under aluminum leaves skinless
wonders tempt wildflowers

Night: along dirt path teardrops fall to
complete darkness

Night: whispers short hosannas

Josh Goldberg

Night: last light in sky moves dark tides
to other side

Night: intoxication centers on sky color
of oblivion

Night: vacant cast-off shells of cicadas

Night: corner of room nestles
scattered nightmares

Night: sudden arrival wrestles the wind

Night: gazes at cloud smoke leaving-returning

Night: moon mute in its veil

A Thousand-and-One-Nights

Night: mouths vowels of chalk

Night: strip the air of shrouds

Night: with salt forgetting how
to face the wind

Night: must belong to pliable chameleons

Night: gritty earth dank an untrimmed grave

Night: revealed squirming

Night: fireflies caught in headlights flicker
in void left behind

Night: bright spots changing constellations

Josh Goldberg

Night: single surface vast embrace three
inches from heart

Night: darkness curves toward light never
comes back

Night: future time buoyed moonless
half melodies

Night: shadow-prophet of his being

Night: deepens eyes distant worlds

Night: quiet in thin spring rain

Night: unlike first-plucked morning-teaspoons

A Thousand-and-One-Nights

Night: mountain fires boast of love

Night: smell of small hearts cooling

Night: hideous grounds come into existence

Night: darkness underpins perfectly still

Night: dream-paths storm-rutted

Night: stiff-wood fantasies snapped-splinters
scatter

Night: lips move refuse names

Night: we cannot see without thinning
the blood

Josh Goldberg

Night: illuminated star-clusters cannot
offer direction

Night: dawn dangles voided worlds

Night: tomorrow-dream aborts light-clarity

Night: slow reach between her legs

Night: heart-cheap promises

Night: vast-swallowing blackness

Night: execution-feigned holiness

Night: glass eyes without pressure-seeing

A Thousand-and-One-Nights

Night: centuries pass with tiny scare-gods

Night: distance conceals deepest sorrow

Night: last eyes nowhere in sight

Night: nearest ear for kindling

Night: cup-full dusk-tinted clouds

Night: half-dark touches more than
the Almighty

Night: unlike Aristotlizing Day

Night: asleep in my sleep

Josh Goldberg

Night: one hour darkness worth twelve of day

Night: turns eyes toward what was first
in world

Night: sacrificial cream on sinking ship

Night: tenderness all futility fills

Night: no sooner than alone

Night: makes one provincial

Night: delicate breeze blows on thin line
of sleep

Night: first dream-language never-understood

A Thousand-and-One-Nights

Night: evening prayers without color
scorches heart

Night: almost-silent kiss

Night: open graves move hands to mouth

Night: overheard insect-chuckles

Night: unable to lose semen
body fails to waken

Night: moonlit-wondrous breasts

Night: lip-by-lip storm

Night: hands around cold cups

Josh Goldberg

Night: lukewarm drizzle slowly returns

Night: just as well talk about nothing

Night: darkness finishes flapping wings

Night: wind blows relentlessly uneven

Night: felt presence above-lip

Night: large eyes of horse

Night: forages rose-wounds

Night: tutelary-shades black-hammers

Night: goodness-freed eye-socket blind

Night: worm-long sweet-blessed

Night: hail holy darkness first born of
millennial tears

Night: abstraction-shivers

Night: twin-created soul-dark

Night: void-won

Night: thorn-light of-enough

Night: darkness-knowing

Josh Goldberg

Night: vengeance-houred

Night: needle-perfect

Night: bone-glistened

Night: drowning-splendor

Night: midnight-wet hands

Night: black-plumed drift

Night: constellated-black dread-persistant

Night: prophet of my being

Night: sorrow-wandering dark-avalanche
light-denying

Night: end-gathered complete

Night: bud-enfolding neck-adorned

Night: between gravity's well heaven's abyss
hineni hineni

Night: half-winged half-am

Night: light-faded living-perishing

Night: blind life quiets gypsy-fiddle

Josh Goldberg

Night: epithalamic-sepulchral

Night: tears of joy crystal pendants
of chandeliers

Night: wide arc midnight stars

Night: mother of nothing

Night: dead-living living-dead

Night: fully-gorged

Night: ancient sea slowly turns

Night: doves and slumber

A Thousand-and-One-Nights

Night: intoxication-barge table-parked

Night: vinegar worm-crawl

Night: great eggs of darkness alongside
kitchen knives

Night: ink of first-created

Night: mediator between spirit-body

Night: vapor-dark Holy Ghost

Night: reluctant-summing

Night: quiet turning ten-thousand mile heart

Josh Goldberg

Night: without flutter

Night: exposing daylight lips

Night: end-point white glass of windows

Night: universe-sewn

Night: long flake of black sail climbing
sunlight's fringe

Night: dark first-order pantocrator

Night: collector of lost hours expectations of
long hair

Night: faces clean-rinsed

A Thousand-and-One-Nights

Night: swells at edge of understanding

Night: mouth beneath eyelids

Night: thaw of unborn

Night: heart—dances loose among pines

Night: unlike dawn-readiness

Night: dark-naked in darker cities

Night: never the thing of afternoons

Night: bottomless swelling adrift shames
of world

Josh Goldberg

Night: urgency underlying embodied
placement

Night: boundary-bending light-failing
black home

Night: city-bred wing-swallowed

Night: in wounds of sleeplessness

Night: abyss beyond dreams eager to love

Night: cold-sure throat-pale

Night: phantom of dubious unfolding

Night: gently tapped fertile egg

A Thousand-and-One-Nights

Night: bright-moon thickets
carbon-imprinted greys

Night: renamed Great Empty

Night: should you die leave front door open

Night: origin of all things hidden yet mad for
horizons

Night: three-pain inches from floor I am
buried in shadow

Night: seated deep on black couch against
white doorway

Night: knit together like an old sweater

Josh Goldberg

Night: arrives chanting prayers

Night: tumbles off the table

Night: peels like fruit

Night: abandons you like
old mattress stuffing

Night: morphine landscape

Night: roaring sea

Night: Tablet of Existence

Night: storm-port port-storm

A Thousand-and-One-Nights

Night: blessing-cloak murderous-secrets

Night: sharp edge of a fairytale

Night: teeth one morning recedes into gums

Night: lips narrow

Night: blackboard to write *impermanent*

Night: great for so-longs

Night: can make all the difference

Night: country without rainbow of deception

Josh Goldberg

Night: territory of unpleasant cats

Night: places of unseen freshness after
late-hour rain

Night: dark-sea miracle in the closet

Night: curves along the spine at twilight

Night: exists as He Himself saw

Night: replaces all vowels

Night: this dream-script this hallucination

Night: how many more sequels?

A Thousand-and-One-Nights

Night: can't spoon off excess or suck it through straw

Night: rejects all except distance

Night: does not twist or turn or circle back but like broken glass exhausts

Night: an almost-tomorrow

Night: write your name beneath it

Night: an un-openable curtain once you look back

Night: shores with deep troughs

Josh Goldberg

Night: dream never lives inside interpretation

Night: real as drops of last summer's rain

Night: always hatchet to the egg's light

Night: hair-shadow humanity

Night: first rectitude-lesson moonlight-folds

Night: hides path to your beauty

Night: last seal of my being

Night: present-ground death-strapped

A Thousand-and-One-Nights

Night: penumbra-wolf back-circles

Night: lays black eggs

Night: blocks all paths to origins
because it is Origin

Night: forgets burned cheekbones
white pupils

Night: ontology-tears of snow

Night: each arriving thought holds
"I am", "night"

Night: dances over sleeping God

Josh Goldberg

Night: ancient essence of wind-rinsed light

Night: alone before ancient battlements
dew-bathed

Night: conversation reveals absurd thinking

Night: darkness concern for last things

Night: possibilities because we misread
what we see

Night: uncontainable-swallow mist-future

Night: wind-broken brightly-grown

Night: springtime of blackest blessedness

A Thousand-and-One-Nights

Night: on all four sides my own wandering

Night: crescent moon pulls children
up by chin

Night: mountain pushes the door open bits of
windows tremble

Night: stone-burnt desert-dark

Night: imagining walk in snow

Night: heart among pillows

Night: I used to see you as ambulant porcelain

Night: now blind like an olive

Night: visiting rain moves toward me like haze

Night: raucous crows recall river-black stones

Night: bitter root of grounding

Night: unlike hostile *hyle* of the world

Night: heavy rain polishes stone in heart

Night: door with no key opens dawn

Night: triggers *pathe* of soul

Night: denies celestial rust our daily bread

A Thousand-and-One-Nights

Night: knots caul around head

Night: not ruinous as lucidity

Night: moon moves along Animus River

Night: salt-sprinkled wisdom-awakened

Night: panic-washed earth-white

Night: wind-carried arms-shuddering

Night: reality-am

Night: here is what is there

Josh Goldberg

Night: fullness etched and polished

Night: far end of desolate hall scorched
air circulates

Night: self-drowning high-tide

Night: drunk-scattered gauze-soaked
flight-broken

Night: unknown mercurial tides

Night: wine returns me to moon
with sound of blood in ears

Night: submit your tracks one by one

Night: why worry about illusion?

Night: what it does not have it gives

Night: what is spent it spends

Night: nothing is *foreign*

Night: at dusk one has meals of silence

Night: distant figures wind slant with
black-marker integrity

Night: rising tides millennia dust

Night: soul moans like a child

Josh Goldberg

Night: her meniscus rocks gently
by open window

Night: branching stars straight up in burls
of momentary oneness

Night: grief burns through the day cool
by bedtime

Night: scratches at the throat of uncertainty

Night: desire joins fingers where they
meet palm

Night: gas-station bathroom in big slow drops

Night: old sneakers against wall lichens
or snow?

Night: sequins baked in moonlight worn
with unknown eyes

Night: countdown-clock bolted to neighbor's
universe-door

Night: in a box with milk chord

Night: lacquered rail bends law of physics
toward satisfaction

Night: pregnant childhood forests magical
moons gone pinwheel

Night: rat wakes up with gesture of spiritual
surrender

Night: saucy cockroach by back door
almost black

Night: doused in soy sauce murder of crows

Night: tire-flat boredom

Night: hardened by highway old mattress's
eye-popping springs

Night: best with frozen snow

Night: corner-rain traps trash-ripened
newborn wads

Night: morning-segue coffee-eggs

Night: day-bone fingers clack away

Night: nothing visible but unplowed awe

Night: expands as windows shrink

Night: Religion of Day low plank-bridge
to setting sun

Night: nothing so much as proximity

Night: unfulfilled promises

Night: untended dogs dead on the chest

Night: tender with dew still kisses conspire

Josh Goldberg

Night: no one lives in peace with sun

Night: does not cut with edge of broken shell
like day

Night: redolent first and last words

Night: reassures when we realize a dark sun

Night: wing-felt star-poised

Night: late mist-walking

Night: listening stops living behind eyelids
begins

Night: certainly one must know love

A Thousand-and-One-Nights

Night: essential like sleep without grammar

Night: dream-cans left open

Night: first waking thought

Night: last conscious thought closes eyes:
rain

Night: skylight-glass scrathing

Night: hair gone white long ago

Night: never elsewhere-daylight

Night: soft lakeside idleness

Night: tender-filled coming-going

Night: God's concealment-awakening

Night: truth-mirror analogies sublime

Night: eye-dark socket-plucked

Night: not measured counted weighed
evaluated anticipated or guessed

Night: Nothingness-pissing

Night: however much you may write you have
not gotten to first page

Night: reality-imperfect world-opposed

A Thousand-and-One-Nights

Night: self-propels each room

Night: turns well-spring circles closed eyes

Night: hand-dark tremblings

Night: beginning-point dark-point

Night: old synagogue windows panic-hours

Night: prowls with cat's step

Night: hammer-day rock-shattered angels
sleep in trees

Night: along curved lines

Josh Goldberg

Night: possibility-charged

Night: discharge-distant voice-called

Night: invisible touch on flesh

Night: paradox-covered rain-love

Night: inhabits stone in palm of hand

Night: infinity-moments pan-fried

Night: black thunder immense tulip

Night: black water white camellia

A Thousand-and-One-Nights

Night: dark farming

Night: stem-level deep

Night: respiration-relentless
alphabet-shattered

Night: daylight-false bed-sad

Night: turns sea into land into sea

Night: people into stranger into people

Night: her tongue joins contraries

Night: love-seen dew-shimmer

Night: bunchgrass-choking

Night: dawn-spoken

Night: cloistered in corporeal eyes

Night: "I am God-Desire"

Night: half-light arrangements

Night: dead escape themselves

Night: naked-felt lust-filled

Night: horizon-eroded devout

A Thousand-and-One-Nights

Night: tyrannized-day coincident-opposite

Night: no true life only melanoid living

Night: clitter-call slow-distant

Night: no demand for legitimacy

Night: covered-over crushed-under

Night: grey melts away candle firefly

Night: known to be mine as well

Night: scours cluster clouds
to edge of extinction

Josh Goldberg

Night: I shelter its breathing body before
the light switch

Night: four walls of house pitched in gloom

Night: special way it removes skin

Night: sublunary blessings

Night: blood-pool scatter snow-baptism

Night: hole bottoms out in agony

Night: savior what you sense

Night: stomach-full blossom-blown

A Thousand-and-One-Nights

Night: lunacy not lacking

Night: with snow sand flurried skies
willow-blossom sense

Night: vacancy-descending

Night: birth-taken womb-dark

Night: moon-side

Night: silence-eating

Night: reason-gnawed abyss-loitered

Night: serrated leaves spin toward dawn

Josh Goldberg

Night: dream-mentor solitude-master

Night: rootless trees in corners of eyes

Night: eclipse-dark mirror-renounced

Night: transcendence approaches
tongue of ash

Night: sustains fraction of myself

Night: broken glass slices sudden splendor

Night: poultice of snakes and literalists

Night: somewhere to hide pain

A Thousand-and-One-Nights

Night: pane-moon brightness-twisted

Night: I am sentience

Night: man of limited dimension

Night: seed in every species

Night: back to me reborn

Night: in abstract arrival

Night: curled up half-asleep
her side of the bed

Night: light shapes failure

Josh Goldberg

Night: weapons raised

Night: accusation-instants

Night: truly delivered

Night: without Novocain

Night: twilight-thick immolations

Night: crimson-throat flames

Night: deep-attachment apocalyptic-cakes

Night: black-flag fronds

A Thousand-and-One-Nights

Night: withdrawn-wordless

Night: first arrive last leave

Night: child in ruined house

Night: lost in another century breath in mouth

Night: end of dirt road weighty autumn

Night: walks back along hard road

Night: beleaguered affection never quite mine

Night: unfolds sad walls clattering memories

Josh Goldberg

Night: unapparent I shape you in the clouds

Night: husbanding light I remove my face

Night: some scars should be left to mercy
of elements

Night: or left alone collecting dust
in waiting rooms

Night: orchid beyond darkness

Night: who shall help disperse spores
open wounds?

Night: road floods your breath in my mouth

A Thousand-and-One-Nights

Night: ill-light perfume-hurricanes

Night: tongue-aware hair-lament

Night: thunder-croaked book-wounded

Night: tornado twists lips at bed's edge

Night: living out our own edge of sky

Night: what else suffers listening to me?

Night: waking up body turns simple

Night: circle-white unsayable unfolds

Josh Goldberg

Night: hateful-angle curtain
mist-smear window

Night: with least suffocation two breasts
of your choice

Night: bone-stained observation

Night: ground-scratched wonders

Night: bitter-hardened I AM-necessity

Night: white-gowned in sleepless tissues

Night: downpour of your name

Night: blast of air sharpens mirror's image

A Thousand-and-One-Nights

Night: broken magnets cast off
by receding refrigerator

Night: light-awakened frugality-afflicted

Night: thread plunges into known world

Night: no saying how this feels
mid-desert moon

Night: shadow-slipped skull-digested

Night: woman crying out in sleep fills my robe

Night: world passes away with sulphur smile

Josh Goldberg

Night: leaden-cluster birds

Night: obscure smile on a bedsheet

Night: everything recovers without loss

Night: manner of seeing butter yellow

Night: pull away daylight scab darkness
still moist

Night: having experienced pain of snow-dust

Night: shudder at falling winter-white down

Night: halls pale as mother's knock-off nylons

A Thousand-and-One-Nights

Night: preternatural sensitivity to slow
factories of desire

Night: raising uncanniness three-feet high

Night: gums ready to host

Night: things at hand world-poor

Night: dead men turn blind eyes sideways

Night: saints become humble blessing axes

Night: crows wish everything black

Night: galaxy eyes with spinning arms

Josh Goldberg

Night: sloughs off self as overlapping circles

Night: pray for nothing then break into run

Night: realize only in half-light the half-sign

Night: half-step into wild grass the key

Night: wine glass clear heat settles

Night: hinge-dismantled imagination

Night: weak as specks of foam

Night: single hair turns fiction into desire

A Thousand-and-One-Nights

Night: specific pull of annihilation-beaches

Night: with blasphemous pitch leaf-screaming
across infinity

Night: barefoot-playing anxieties

Night: road from airport littered with
avocados women in orange dresses

Night: birds in flight over weeds of poverty

Night: body unlocks like curled scorpion

Night: is there a softer side of suicide?

Night: old goat stricken with gid

Josh Goldberg

Night: tongue to the roof dark
planting waiting

Night: to dewdrop mind iron trees
extend branches

Night: not even slightest indication
of her breast

Night: brain restricted to chemistry mind
to exigent angels

Night: ask the embryo about tiger's teeth

Night: heart knocks against dreadful void

Night: stuttering best way to read Torah

A Thousand-and-One-Nights

Night: tender spaces clawed by panther
in the corner

Night: investigate inflating doorways
flooding cellars

Night: moon-sharp razor-glare

Night: fountain-black irises dark-sky dreaming

Night: neck kiss at close range

Night: endless rounds raw dying

Night: moonlight on ground frost on bed

Night: oar-strokes through the house

Josh Goldberg

Night: keep going keep going

Night: tonight's living eyes elsewhere

Night: between forks of lightning
in hell with you

Night: blessed is she blessed is she
in spite of herself can see

Night: snow sleeps lightly as wounded bird

Night: tender-meat dusk-red

Night: nothing so much raises blessedness as
hair standing on end

A Thousand-and-One-Nights

Night: having nothing but blissful singularity

Night: love beaten by Spring

Night: God winks to God behind each of us

Night: free of shrines black eyes
saturate your robe

Night: recognize what is hidden so it can be
clear to you

Night: awakening you destroy the world

Night: messianic women church-dark
possibilities

Josh Goldberg

Night: screaming-upright cat-desire

Night: sewer-drawn flesh-spasms

Night: nothing left but what's coming

Night: nothing need be said the tiled moon

Night: sleep arrives gently through window
with warm wind

Night: crow's belly hidden by wing-sheaths

Night: blue-day tomorrows set in crystal

Night: light fades listening to heads rolling
on roof

A Thousand-and-One-Nights

Night: faith depends upon the ear

Night: lightning flashes dissipates
sweat-smelling underwear

Night: last Jew plays on a tibia slips over curve
of the world

Night: boxcar-empty cantilena-slow

Night: astral salt on posthumous lakes

Night: crow's snow deepens solitude

Night: God walks backwards restoring world's
wild drifting

Josh Goldberg

Night: confession of bones makes one shutter

Night: lightning's-vein horizon's desert

Night: attached to illusion a thousand wires

Night: corner mirror shakes out
sad midday dust

Night: winter wind sings its ephemeral miracle

Night: wind-grief open-window

Night: eye briny with sea gazing

Night: before Adam contained Eve

A Thousand-and-One-Nights

Night: hollows out anticipation

Night: slurs a pause

Night: eye-blind belly hungers

Night: non-believing devourer

Night: incident of shapes in an empty field

Night: penumbra-cellar disintegration-self

Night: eggs boil rain cries

Night: evening ghosts arise from pores

Josh Goldberg

Night: lake's wan face collects on wet clothes

Night: recalibrates senses sidereal-regret

Night: star-thickened window-blessed

Night: endless-multiplicity homeward-limp

Night: whirlwind rotating on small hinge

Night: deep-sleeve alchemy

Night: empty cistern pale in light
of uncertain hours

Night: sugar of your tongue
a succulent charity

A Thousand-and-One-Nights

Night: eyes double at the window

Night: your fur coast discharges small storms

Night: shared-horizon algorithms

Night: aboriginal beginnings curl

Night: toss of fireflies

Night: stones appear-disappear lightning flash

Night: past plunders itself

Night: wind's edge touches silver glass

Josh Goldberg

Night: nocturnal circus never far

Night: bread-hardened corpse-saint

Night: Holy Ghost of pale trembling

Night: Altar of Black Dogs

Night: fills elliptical galaxies odd angles
coin-operated doors

Night: joy-innocence of tin mines

Night: divine-debris salivating-harps

Night: lips wet with china cup

A Thousand-and-One-Nights

Night: rain beats on roof the song
of great peace

Night: dance between bodies

Night: sooner or later salt in air cracks gums

Night: broken alley weeds glyphs of God

Night: blind child opens eyes

Night: naked-quiet

Night: moonbeam-delirium

Night: wolf smile an open bedroom ash-dark

Josh Goldberg

Night: asymmetrical body wind-driven soft

Night: telepathic summer destroy
tomorrow's passenger

Night: wounds rather than kisses?

Night: insufficiency unties glory-tongue

Night: god's un-capitalized head

Night: overripe eyes on your woman's body

Night: distant lightning sharpens heat
a horse-eye to the rain

Night: this moment dime-thin

Night: Time spreads his thighs

Night: straw-dog darkness-covered

Night: disappointment-droplets

Night: the Before stillborn

Night: Jesus rises backward in form of Torah

Night: no air motion yet overhead fan

Night: at end everything reborn
immense staircases

Night: razor-smile on pumpkin face

Josh Goldberg

Night: late shadows occasional bird-wing

Night: unsuspected domains
unpretentious auditoria

Night: embracing wetness reabsorbed rain

Night: song-slept silk of perfect meaning

Night: caught between mock sovereignties

Night: moment of grace grey mouse
slides off roof

Night: God laughs among ruins

Night: empty skull weathers autumn

A Thousand-and-One-Nights

Night: dusk-manna blood-porridge

Night: trees chloroform-quiet

Night: sheets soaked ash-trays smell of tin

Night: dark-spotted hands ember eyes

Night: sunset clocks hiccup untrue words
move toward another

Night: world leaves as it arrives
hummingbird-swift

Night: burning dark suddenly free
likes-dislikes

Josh Goldberg

Night: winter's ash-horizon

Night: horse soaks in evening rain eyes alive
having reached salvation

Night: anonymous streets accompanying
my absence

Night: stray dog-man

Night: seizes world imposed on it

Night: under the pretext of utility
I have chosen Thou

Night: summer heat fly upside-down on
ceiling knives cold on floor

A Thousand-and-One-Nights

Night: white tablecloth still as dead
glass of water

Night: in-house objects wait for light as winter
waits for spring

Night: marked by fatal reverie rooster
crows at dawn

Night: thunder-point amen-prayer

Night: hips of wasp move toward
the tiled bathroom

Night: hunting my own blood

Night: moves like honey in a glass bowl

Josh Goldberg

Night: tooth cracks on bone cat leaps down
from chair

Night: sepulchral smiles exhausted stone
torsos

Night: pecked by rain two beautiful legs

Night: doorway squatters' pale-blue
stone-eyes

Night: Torah of the Void *sola scriptura*

Night: wineglasses at dusk prolegomena
reflections

Night: enucleated eye foreshortens wound

A Thousand-and-One-Nights

Night: inaccessible shadows shot with silken
hues ancient skies

Night: moon's wiped-away dark-hand cloud

Night: hemp-rope thick after rain
bones thin as summer air

Night: city bathes high-tide in moonlight
buttocks mid-way to standing

Night: exaggeration of clean laundering goat's
scrotum

Night: violin's high pitch above quay
of the dead

Night: angels end their lives if seeds ripen
under skirts

Night: copulating dog boner
in place of presence

Night: names that bend knees ignites death

Night: woman laughing her waist appears

Night: breasts color of warm milk I have not
yet grown weary

Night: tapeworm washed in moonlight

Night: snow idles mid-air voices dimly heard

A Thousand-and-One-Nights

Night: I-among things roll circumspectly

Night: an egg devoid of axis

Night: wind flings large leaves neighbor's dog
pisses on mailbox

Night: collective hallucinations require
shared tongues

Night: dogs snatches air hungry ghosts
swallow wind

Night: whir of low wings wakefulness of coitus

Night: ambiguous heart itself under *tallit*

Josh Goldberg

Night: far away white pupils open certain
kind of mouth

Night: "keep vomiting to live" has certain
ring to it

Night: throat smells of bleach

Night: laid alongside horse's penis
farmer's apples

Night: slowly with spoon she gags on roses

Night: losing the path rain on hard stones

Night: I gargle the milk of blessings

A Thousand-and-One-Nights

Night: I set fire to the looted contours
of false identities

Night: I pin grace to your lapel
to sweeten your fate

Night: salvation's hard like a plaster fetus

Night: dark winter sky slices bone-quick

Night: buttock's slow shudder she floats
over my head

Night: nails stick out from walls the dark
wingspan of nightmares

Night: long moments soak deeply into dusk
as I lose form

Josh Goldberg

Night: men quietly covered in pale sulphur

Night: reach of angels between zero
and infinity

Night: tomatoes on the window sill dim
in soft dusk's haze

Night: cracked-open piddocks un-bandage
long-held heat

Night: sowing rapture's seas against
raw-smelling wind

Night: into to the center of a dark kiss
splashed with blood

A Thousand-and-One-Nights

Night: soft bones rounded with sleep

Night: swallowing desire's tiny eggs we fall
in love to be naked

Night: dusk-thighs expose white-hard
porcelain bowl

Night: sorrow-region sliding dark

Night: canvas commits suicide not the painter

Night: last fart before bed looking
straight ahead

Night: you are not here you were never here
wind-bells hang silent

Josh Goldberg

Night: digs into the open eye of daylight
without changing her pose

Night: what would daybreak's nail say?

Night: winks from corner where the answer
to knowing lies?

Night: summer arrives spilling liquid gold
across the desert

Night: first dark spit of rain
a single glass of wine

Night: hides his torment with
an artist's grey eraser

Night: edgeless wound the size of an embrace

A Thousand-and-One-Nights

Night: another child sluices into the world

Night: love screams in dull places

Night: heavy-bent sadness collapses
like cardboard roof

Night: hides the secret *nothing*

Night: just say "the lower half of her breasts"

Night: will half-ripe flesh remain fresh
in winter?

Night: growing old and crazy *duende* yawns
in the studio

Josh Goldberg

Night: clitoris calls the slow dew on grass

Night: bathed in orchid water alone
I view the moon

Night: at bottom of the bottle seeing willows

Night: sometimes the soul tries to squeeze
out of body like toothpaste

Night: under Thou-roofs men spill quietly

Night: my father is reborn next spin of the sky

Night: titanium gloves the pallor of a face

A Thousand-and-One-Nights

Night: still mountains sound of puddles
fingers grasp the hand

Night: thigh bones whistle "You"

Night: mole-cricket above me painfully in love

Night: stitch eye under the tongue
so you'll understand

Night: white eye on brackish pond

Night: on edge of open wound

Night: her fire-black rose washes child's neck

Night: flight of bats shakes the tambourine

Josh Goldberg

Night: under black heel of thought
milky half-light

Night: clandestine words catch on alien spurs

Night: bits of your skin in my heart

Night: my steady throat gathers birds

Night: blood spills sponges dipped
in hot water

Night: feet in the fur of cat summer
fills the room

Night: sleep of splintered weeping world of
bones ran out of fat

A Thousand-and-One-Nights

Night: rain rushes to the lungs
corroding incisions

Night: I scrape across the white arch
of your belly

Night: I alone bleach your bones

Night: fly chases the hand a single bed sleeps
with someone

Night: lost among broken shadows I am the
Northern Dipper

Night: place-holder of our
mysterium tremendum

Josh Goldberg

Night: cold birds caught in caul
of frosted glass

Night: ordinary people expectorate
many ghosts

Night: stronger for being unspoken
rain clouds darkly-deep

Night: words end tongue on floor

Night: inside just herself rinsing hair
with snowflakes

Night: two breasts nurse single halo

Night: star-light's shuddering-tracks

A Thousand-and-One-Nights

Night: under linen sky twilight-wells a single
poem falls through autumn air

Night: gnat stuck between the teeth I should
remember my parents

Night: thorn-oak splits the
tongue dialog begins

Night: memory of French feminine *e*

Night: glowing embers among possessions

Night: last summer's dead fly under the
calendar

Night: distant thunder cracks the clock rolls
tongue back into its darkness

Josh Goldberg

Night: sister plum indigestible as stone

Night: when it came back to see me it circled
my face with solitude

Night: high-pitch crickets rub the
universe's legs

Night: sacrifice like sex performed many ways

Night: useless as a hanged man
with an erection

Night: shadows bend walls guests gaze
at each other

Night: black bureau old woman unmoving
during the storm

A Thousand-and-One-Nights

Night: lamp only what it needs

Night: moon-viewing
glowing lawn stakes swollen

Night: burnt toast at dusk empty cicada-shell
soon forgotten

Night: eve of another year lost trajectory
of bullet

Night: black-sky mirror skirt-shining stars

Night: self-absorption once cold swoons warm

Night: neighbors eat way toward sleep

Josh Goldberg

Night: awakening nameless corpses sentenced
to hard labor

Night: jagged edges breathe soon dry

Night: only eyes reflect lamp in dark room

Night: adding canceling multiplying realities
winter ice

Night: what cannot be heard the
evanescence's hiss

Night: forgotten as lining in old hat living with
the right source

Night: wind at the sea's end inside this fog

A Thousand-and-One-Nights

Night: egg faces moon

Night: thinly sliced in search of larger
proposition

Night: with the hum of stars under neighbor
leaves

Night: skies soft as merino wool

Night: darkness erases itself under bed my
bad habits

Night: sniff of sour milk image of blue snow

Night: dead frog waits for rain besides
casuarina grove

Josh Goldberg

Night: tufts of white flowers wash away ash
of sorrow

Night: brackish moonscape broken factory
roofs double-family flats

Night: chain-link fence swings gate pitted by
salt air

Night: weedy back lots lost fathers who
never cared

Night: stuffed cockatoo falls on own eye
summer storm ends

Night: low rumblings prefigure shattering

Night: gray rump sack under water

A Thousand-and-One-Nights

Night: childhood hides inside roof beams

Night: last leavening remembrances laid-out
like potsherds

Night: in abandoned gardens wasted
dark-forevers

Night: rain-glaze on empty streets moves
dead leaves

Night: wing-black moonlight-flecked

Night: storefront windows reflect solitary
girls' pale forehead shadows

Night: corner of temple kills with eyes of
inlaid silver

Josh Goldberg

Night: heart doesn't yearn flowers but songs

Night: rinses away sun's midday slant

Night: dark embroiderer breaks her fast brings things to life

Night: Player pumps His black harmonium

Night: morning frames presence as desert frames absence

Night: iced shrimp beneath our blankets

Night: cleaves bone to flesh tongue to teeth

Night: fist on the sand in between no image

A Thousand-and-One-Nights

Night: solders air to void cats to cartons

Night: I am re-begot

Night: pulse chases nothing but itself

Night: God-free no one to call

Night: unnamed murmurings forms soft nests

Night: in the state of rubber smokestacks
birth naked figures

Night: taste of anise bitter on your tongue

Night: soul-retching without loss of faith

Josh Goldberg

Night: black lilacs light your eyes

Night: heart scatters mind fire-guts

Night: line-thin charcoal-lonely

Night: nose-drop heavy at tip old body flickers

Night: white-flow on fingertips

Night: stones in mouth turn words
like calendars

Night: *corpora non agunt nisi fluida*

Night: wild-swells walled-in

Night: sin an imprisoned conceit

Night: immensity taps the window

Night: blissfully slides down into sinkhole
of myself

Night: redeemed by forgiveness dry diet
of my burning

Night: maelstrom gives birth to wind-child

Night: heart-blossom Buddha's drowsy eyes

Night: small heads at the window

Night: as if never born

Josh Goldberg

Night: last year haunts our looks

Night: tips of your eyelashes with side of
butter beans

Night: house crickets age naked bodies

Night: I am being dreamed by you are you
being dreamed by me?

Night: last light milkweed tornados

Night: cat ears in the underwear

Night: glimpse of overripe fruit by
walking-stick

A Thousand-and-One-Nights

Night: suddenly dinner plates slide under foot

Night: sips whiskey writes poems

Night: sky remembers hawk-shuddered kill

Night: for a while she is visible question of
extended hands

Night: friends nowhere sighting
welcome mats

Night: pregnant lips resplendent with orgasms

Night: hot water overflow reassures
open senses

Josh Goldberg

Night: first moaning is for you mouth
suddenly enormous for me

Night: just about every backyard desire

Night: bends over sound of fallen leaves

Night: human hair meets impulse of lust

Night: first shadows then eggs leave temple

Night: cremation ashes pause in descent

Night: carbon evenings flower moonrise

Night: clouding doorway flint of your forehead

A Thousand-and-One-Nights

Night: words said in order to exist

Night: urinating love

Night: low sink water certain kind of hair

Night: shapes of our impermanence

Night: heavy gusts inside rainy season close

Night: slum-specks moon's sky bridges
bone-white

Night: fine grain hearts small toy boxes

Night: tiny fates uncaring floods
of viscous matter

Josh Goldberg

Night: insect intermediaries laughingly rich
sleep with dogs

Night: humanity full-blown infection

Night: outliers by every measure

Night: necks contort to steel lights undazzled
by naked cat

Night: trapped between old losses those
newly arriving

Night: in large dark smudge scarce flowers
grow dark

Night: sudden standstill of hummingbirds
enduring summer

A Thousand-and-One-Nights

Night: fallen hairpins on crystalline floors

Night: rage-shaped to comprehend soul

Night: without turning back sound of trees

Night: pain's gray light the early dragonfly

Night: worm holes in old star charts
heaven's sieve

Night: after-rain steam moonlight on
neglected road

Night: ash-rain falls at which point
we again *know*

Josh Goldberg

Night: waiting for morning's *cryptica scriptura*

Night: in next life's round perhaps I will be
better looking

Night: *I* do not grow in the sun

Night: my face cedar bark beyond
windowpane

Night: tongue-less you speak to me leg-less
I walk into your room

Night: do I slander you by exaggeration?

Night: small rooms unhurt parts

A Thousand-and-One-Nights

Night: surrounded by scissors distaste for
things close

Night: ground-scattered Palo Verde blossoms
turn more yellow

Night: hair-shedding cat settles into place

Night: don't hold your breath while dancing

Night: at sixth extinction forget pawnshops

Night: sit in chair alone with a book

Night: for non-believers scrambled eggs
with lox

Josh Goldberg

Night: soundtrack in head low-volume
self-preservation

Night: God hunts Himself

Night: don't misjudge sleeping cats

Night: post-rapture villainy hard-travelling
midnight scurry

Night: riverbed crows silent before storm

Night: place livens up with dead friends

Night: eyelids cold with color of plaster

A Thousand-and-One-Nights

Night: in control-freak territory
with instant coffee

Night: Holy Spirit jumps out of bed

Night: snowstorms head south for winter

Night: necktie dangles like frogs' legs

Night: pale horizon raises quiet conversations

Night: distance-losing voices headed
by two children

Night: old woman's smile creates
ghost mother

Josh Goldberg

Night: dreaming sunflower thickets
in autumn wind

Night: indifferent forces quickly forgotten

Night: no going no coming the ruined
clay house

Night: just ten directions of *thusness*

Night: absence sits by the lake shore

Night: speckled-moon wild-heart the groin
turns inside-out

Night: ignorant of resurrection wall-eyed
cat sits here

A Thousand-and-One-Nights

Night: intimate words separate like
swallows in love

Night: finish dying then come back to me

Night: empathy lacquered on black metal

Night: summer heat with small cuts

Night: late-in-the-life moon becomes larger
just breathing

Night: ticking grows louder ordained by blood

Night: in the dark regardless of rain

Josh Goldberg

Night: blade of presence slices through
nonsense in head

Night: dark lake of stillness raindrops
fall soundlessly

Night: void isn't where to knock

Night: in shadow of electric pole hundred
grass blades

Night: facing my shadow making friends

Night: hiking back down trail toasting
full moon

Night: one eye opens to deeper grace

A Thousand-and-One-Nights

Night: ladle out another moon

Night: when all's empty clarity of rain
sweeps in

Night: tiny mist-droplets love's urination

Night: at the edge of insanity trust yourself

Night: half-caring half not-caring

Night: trees sob without salt or moon

Night: clear crisp moon don't hoard your
heart away

Night: no reply from bed I pool dark shadows

Josh Goldberg

Night: long corridor unfolds like unlined paper

Night: prison or not clear light
daybreak arrives

Night: dishwasher aches erotic
something-more

Night: limitless rain ill-fitting tooth

Night: buttery egg slips through the world

Night: lost knife in my hand evening afterglow

Night: carrying out junk I carried out love
by mistake

A Thousand-and-One-Nights

Night: rug on floor of empty room with
no name

Night: nocturnal face births my own
resemblance

Night: newly-found self-awareness between
buttocks and chair

Night: flesh quivers at call

Night: erotic liquefaction what did
she awaken?

Night: tongues adorn your hair

Night: hidden at bed's horizon thighs
of wet nurse

Night: buds under your arms yield place
to live

Night: intoxicated your hand lost-and-found

Night: far-travelling penis sends its seed aloft

Night: neglected water twig-high

Night: soul is wheel rolling on cloud

Night: shadows on snow fall across lap

Night: mouth open in corner of kitchen the
brilliant moon

Night: perfume necks blue from strangulation

A Thousand-and-One-Nights

Night: sand mixing with memories of you

Night: her left hand coils with interruptions

Night: two hands held out reflect nothing

Night: to explain one thing already
missed point

Night: moon's brightness sweeps
backyard clean

Night: laughter arises from cistern
drenched with spray

Night: gnat set within frame nothing
in house to drink

Josh Goldberg

Night: half-ghosts bite us now and then

Night: damp grass pales I go to eat silence

Night: household items diamond ornaments
dead bones your breath of new life

Night: words waste away shed blood
by window

Night: much easier to die licking off stars

Night: two dimples on face embrace
everything

Night: lepers hang like melancholy bells dead
age like whiskey

A Thousand-and-One-Nights

Night: breasts seen through wine-glass
the chill rain

Night: goes into the next room robbed
of bloom

Night: staircase broken imagination folds

Night: lengthy aspirated *h*

Night: clock-side crisis tomorrowfull sky

Night: caulked words pause before coffin

Night: arrives with a crutch under its wing

Night: cobweb against my ribs

Josh Goldberg

Night: kisses white bone starts to snow

Night: chowder in glass bowl old
downtown restaurant

Night: smoke gives form to wind potted
flowers arranged in row

Night: light will grow on any dunghill

Night: existence burns from center outward

Night: her face unmoving under full moon

Night: under blood-arch cobwebs
in early autumn

A Thousand-and-One-Nights

Night: excess shade of summer fruit shatters
my pride

Night: thought of tomorrow's lips squat
around house

Night: summer skyward on a dark road cat
wanting to die

Night: thought of soft frogs the
school lavatory

Night: faint profile of woman under
the roof-ridge

Night: self-deception limitless

Night: wind between arms wife repairs
bright shirt

Josh Goldberg

Night: symmetry congeals irony

Night: solitariness of single pillows

Night: bright side of your breast

Night: soft-boiled egg breakfast-breeze

Night: cat dies on the rug never praying for
happiness of others

Night: content with scent of storm

Night: soul rests like dog at feet

Night: pinches cicada silent

A Thousand-and-One-Nights

Night: faraway trucks bring morning light

Night: heavy clouds sitting by cracked wall

Night: quietly lighting inside-eyes
passing-storm

Night: ground of my being crawls out moist

Night: tree in yard smells dark

Night: wash-water gutter-flow who will swim?

Night: glass of wine thins soft breeze

Night: in storm's leaning light toothbrush
looks big

Josh Goldberg

Night: diesel oil floods irises of eyes with
same cold fever

Night: wind stops world floats
soundlessly about

Night: end of day birds slowly mirrored in
granddaughter's eyes

Night: this spring too shoes darken

Night: moon tangled in your hair cold
against face

Night: between pages of book squashed
gnat lives

A Thousand-and-One-Nights

Night: tree moves gently snake leaves the wall

Night: walking home headlights decay

Night: splintered wrecks daffodil-stuffed
last year's mattress

Night: deep in cup of Presence

Night: autumn ends drawing in India ink

Night: thunder-storm complete single eye
stands upright

Twenty-Four Days

In Place of Knowing

Toward morning's birth having passed the night in a wild bird feeder, stepping over the bright patches of new sunlight on the white wool rug, we move outside into the light quiet as cotton camels seeking roses instead of answers.

1.
Not as precise as a chemist's pipe.
The effort to see ourselves.

More like that plink of water.

Or, feeling the mouth moving.
Out in the high fields beyond dawn.

2.
Chalk beds pale in the cold.
Nothing to dream. Nothing to wake up to.

Just to wake up to dream . . .

Beyond the territorial boundaries of the lungs.
To fly with different wings.

Preface to *Twenty-Four Days*

3.
Away from the black well of space.
High enough to see the boat's small circular path.

Even in the most banal moments.

Looking at all those insoluble loose ends.
With the eye of introspective lye.

— J.G.

1. A Forest of Clouds

1.

The forest of clouds above the brow.
That seems to listen.

Glistens the side-hustle.

Lips suffer exhaustion.
Blathering about nothing in particular.

2.

Imagine a world.
Where reality is open.

Where everything becomes Being.

Setting in play the circle.
Part to whole and back.

3.

If our thoughts were in the palm of the hand.
What would they feel like?

Twenty-Four Days

Sharp as a tooth, moist like a punched eye?

Sand-dissolving the moment of reconciliation?
Less than complete sentences?

2. Adapting to New Conditions

1.
The look of loss.
A folding chair in a church basement.

But I lie.

As I lay myself at the abundance.
A single flower.

2.
May God destroy them.
Those that cannot imagine the night.

Spongy with deadfall.

The tiny whites of my eyes rise up.
Bleeding through higher dimensions.

3.

If you want your meat and potatoes
little one, she says.

Opening the closet.

Full of bats and spikes.
You have to bear your burden.

4.

Never enough holes.
So settle on a spot.

Using your auger test it.

The thick ice on your head.
Softens when the sun begins to rise.

3. After Summer Bath
(The Japanese Print)

Below the cold plate.
Her stomach.

Twenty-Four Days

Dark shadow. Soft wetness.

Sleep gently arrives.
Window. Night wind.

4. Angel of Infinite Faces

1.

Shorthand divine.
Without flicker or flame.

The Angel of Infinite Faces.

Fastening on to your hand.
Gloriously shatters into infinity.

2.

Its shape might be a shape.
Or, substance that shadow seems.

Sweeps away the ground of darkness.

With the look of human understanding.
Terrible as the revelation of Hell.

3.

Below the thunders of the upper deep.
Above dreamless, uninvaded sleep.

Sunlight tugs lightly at the neck.

The Angel of Infinite Faces.
With the softest twist, my swollen eyelids lift.

5. *Archaeological Morning*

1. Focus

Digs, digs round in the ground.
Grief confers obligations.

His tender tie to dreaded bliss.

Centuries deep within the heart.
A middle-yard's worm.

Twenty-Four Days

2. Focus
A dog in the mist of morning.
The Face of daylight.

Stands out against death. Against silence.

Lowers its head.
Until the task complete.

3. Focus
The white sun invests the further-down.
One eye, head half-crowned.

Soon his travels on earth a dream.

Human bones and house-beams.
The uncontained darkness fully-grown.

6. Ash Line

Winter of the following year.
Lightning-flashes dissipate.

Josh Goldberg

Trains travel by moonlight.
Along the ash line through heavy rain.

Last Jews are down-belted.
Empty boxcars the slow cantilena.

Play on found tibias.
Slip over the curve of the world.

7. Atlantic City

1.
Here is where the story ends.
As it should: at the beginning.

At the sight of a stark window-sill.

A zoetrope of days and ways.
The safe cribbing of even bars.

2.
Here is where the story ends.
Hands in back pockets, years unknown
        to be lived.

Twenty-Four Days

A hundred hungry heads torn from the sand.

Baked well to a deep color.
Showing the multitudes how to open
      their eyes.

3.

Here is where the story ends.
Sand-limned processions out from the sea.

Returning reshaped slightly skyward.

The bittersweet awe left behind.
In danger of being forever lost.

8. Cosmic Ocean

I've been in the cosmic ocean.
Seen the True Form.

Faith happened as I was told.

Sooner or later the salt water.
The sleeping snow.

9. Dark Souls

1.

They only come out at night.
Dead souls with little hands.

Sit in salon chairs straightening wet hair.

Glutinous surfaces shining like grave wax.
Drowned out by their own ammoniac tang.

2.

Lungs re-expanded.
Clicks and shifts in the chest.

They start talking. Shaking off cosmic dust.

About television, astral years, the wish to dream.
Exuding odd letters and salty saliva.

3.

Dead souls that never knew
    the treasures concealed.
Within the heart-shaped crater.

Twenty-Four Days

Eyes before and behind. Evening prayer.

Swifts at dusk. A fauna of mirrors.
Insults reborn as sea-monsters.

10. Eater of the Dead

1.

In the dark palimpsest of curling vines.
Touched by the erasure of the
    late afternoon sun.

The ancient portrait on the high nursery wall.

With saliva, bits of straw, and dung.
A filigree drawing on a corpse:
    the Eater of the Dead.

2.

With braided hair hanging on high.
Or twisting long along the floor.

We might have been saved from its
    slinking shadow.

If we had not bitten the newly arrived
        in the world.
Or disturbed the end of time.

3.

The Eater of the Dead is spangled
        like a decaying dream.
A false desire snared by its sweet smell.

Until the next wave of hope appears
        at the horizon.

The storm of black blood will be chased
        by the wind.
Shattering asylum and glimmerland.

11. Flies

1.

Warm weather flies.
On the cover of the trash bin.
Very still..... Meditating.

Cast small shadows weird to life.

2.

Destiny is theirs, ours.
Beyond the flesh of the rose. And flower-fall.

Thus they go about. About.

Seeking knowledge of things past.
On the prow of God's lip.

12. I Saw Myself in a Sequence of Events

I saw myself in a sequence of events.
Walking across the floor at night.

Mite-ridden cracking like peanut shells.

The little grotto at the bottom of the loo.
The shore of an embracing crowd.

13. Layil, or Night

1.
Waking up in the abandoned garden.
He barely hears the voices.

Of his glittering half-children.

He will borrow a thousand eyes to weep with.
For it is always like this: chewing tin.

2.
Shoulders shaking down to the ribs.
A shape coiled in woods and waters.

Ashes in the wind.

Now a tall silent woman.
Her long black hair worn loose.

3.
Unhealed, untreated.
What she flees she takes with her.

Night, her widening thighs.

Twenty-Four Days

An uneven-tempered discourse.
Sin against the King of Glory.

14. Love Poem
(To my Be)

1.
I devour the sun and moon for you.
So tell me you want me.

I am marked by a curious instinct.

I love you whether I want to or not.
I call to you in the voice of the wind.

2.
This body is neither invisible nor intangible.
Far stranger than laughing in my sadness.

The kind of heartache-image for storytellers.

The space just beyond my mouth.
Burn me with a smoldering splinter.

3.

Tell me that you need me.
Tell me that you want me.

Not in ice-light. Under warm nighttime
        river lamps.

On the sad shores bordering the
        inhabited world.
When breezes bring us flood pulse
        and drowning.

15. Parallel Instances

1.

The long day settles in the bones.
Advances toward dusk.

Night is released without a word.

I roll over many times before sleep.
My breath reeling out smoke signals.

2.

Streams within inlets shift.
I am lost and exposed as the weather
        turns bad.

With a sea anchor attached to a rope.

An unknown flower drops into the Nothing.
Unable to blossom for a thousand years.

3.

Canal and tower.
The sound of a pelvis clicking.

Hair of upraised underarms.

Dim and sorted this is not the real world.
The face in the mirror already changed.

16. Pesach

1.

Enter the inner court of the Temple.
Brown earth turns to green.

Josh Goldberg

We offer our skin once more.

And rise like an empty field.
Fat on winter wool.

2.

Studded with soaring towers.
Arrayed with golden adornments.

When too close to the street of butchers.

To the womb-combers.
We break bone and egg.

3.

Under the full moon.
We are still here.

Blood on doorposts: the root of our speech.

Angels showing up with red feet.
Popping veins of blue vipers.

17. Remember
(For my Father)

1.

Can you remember for me?
What I didn't think?

Or what I was not able to remember for myself?

Preoccupy me with the mystery of Time.
The beauty in a stranger's face.

2.

Please remember for me.
Joint or limb of my broken body.

The all-too distinguishable shadow I cast.

The angel's face that has neither face nor eyes.
But my eyes full round about them.

3.

Is there anything you remember?
The slanting sun touching my hand?

How I might swallow all of creation?

An uneaten pastry's cream?
The six dimensions of space?

18. Succubus

1.

I followed the equator.
To the center of the dark kiss.

Down the cool air of caves.

To the soft bones.
Rounded with sleep.

2.

I came on bent elbows.
A child listening.

Swallowing the tiny eggs of night.

Tilting with fullness.
Having eaten, you watched me.

19. Tale of Woe
(Leidensgeschichte)

1.

There was a time.
When we killed only gods.

Now even the spaces between
        houses are dead.

Not even a side-hustle. Finding nothing more.
Than a Once That Never Was.

2.

Greatly devoted to our young.
A child poisoned by a snake.

We bathe in its blood.

Such a world. Such a world.
The darkness under water our foundation.

3.

Claws bind the body to language.
A new hymn arises. Floats in on itself.

As ashes lie wordlessly in dreams.

A crooked grey finger.
The rainstorm that has never been forgiven.

20. The Bite of Resurrection
(For William)

1.

A friend went walking.
Silence his companion.

Among the mountain silver and sky blue.

Only grasshopper and bee his thread.
Tall in grass and wind.

2.

However long the tether.
The glad suffering soul deep in the Garden.

Waiting. For the bite of resurrection.

Twenty-Four Days

Coming to him alone.
Looping through forest reserve and
      lavender field.

3.

His soul's ghostly fog lifted.
And so, these days only season and observer.

Being at this Once.

Nevermore translating sunrise.
At dusk growing an inward landscape.

21. The Great Illusion

1.

We've never been out of "narrow straits".
Egypt has always been in the abandoned room.

In the park with siblings. Ready to embrace
      a new idea.

In unused silences. In each gesture of
        turning away.
Reconstituted like tacky plastic toys.

2.

Why rather than anyone else should
        we own it?
Why this rather than some other thing?

Words turn inside out in order to stay the same.

What happens if they die? Just like that.
Would you be like me?

3.

Sitting on the knees the beast neither fears
        nor pursues.
Sits staring like a purring cat, for now.

Remaining faithful to the family that
        brought it up.

Sometimes I laugh when it sniffs around me.
Winding itself between my legs.

22. The Great Nada

1.

Somewhere between desire and the
        space underneath.
Lies the Great Nada.

Attached like a spider's web on all four corners.

To escape go and do nothing for a while.
To wake up put your finger through it.

2.

The Great Nada.
Has no confusing directions.

Not even a water silence you can take to bed.

You can't scrub it but you can drown in it.
Like a crisp week in November.

3.

The Great Nada.
Lives in the House of Being.

Beyond what is said there is nothing.

An image on the retina of what is not.
An echo of babble uncaring of time.

23. *The World Turns Inside Out*

1.
The world turns inside out.
You just haven't noticed.

Pour me a glass of wine.

I am on a drunken journey.
Playing with colored marbles.

2.
A lonely clothesline.
Unlined blocks of white sandstone.

A corrugated tin fence smiles crookedly.

There's always something left unsaid.
Let's speak familiar things while still
        on the outside.

3.

Once I was home in both worlds.
Braided myself past rust flakes and wastewater.

Listened to women sing of love.

Now at night the heart is beyond the half-wall.
In the early morning the sun is wet-wiped.

24. This is Us

This is us.
Now the deep has opened.

Marking the place where language was lost.

We have swallowed the world.
Without straying from a fixed place.

2.

This is us.
Honed in the darker spaces of dark wood.

Josh Goldberg

Faintly screaming somewhere in its depths.

We've retired the cantos of the imagination.
And stole the food set aside for the dead.

3.
Down, down beneath the grade.
Beneath the burnt-timber and caliche.

Miners drop through time with lamps
        of incongruence.

In our own true world is where we want to be.
Under sewers, in darkness, speaking
        the language of moles.

JOSH GOLDBERG is a poet, translator of Japanese, essayist, book critic, and visual artist. His artwork can be seen at Davis Dominguez Gallery in Tucson, at Susan Street Fine Art in Solana Beach, California, and at joshgoldbergtucson. com. His books of poetry, *A Beggar at the Door: Longer and Shorter Psalms* and *Eight Beggars: Concatenating Verses of Separation and Repair* were also published by Albion-Andalus Books. He lives in Tucson, Arizona.

www.ingramcontent.com/pod-product-compliance
Lightning Source LLC
LaVergne TN
LVHW041154080426
835511LV00006B/598